Young
Thomas Jefferson

Young Thomas Jefferson

by Francene Sabin
illustrated by Robert Baxter

Troll Associates

Library of Congress Cataloging in Publication Data

Sabin, Francene.
  Young Thomas Jefferson.

    Summary: Recounts the life of the versatile inventor
and statesman who became third president of the United
States, with an emphasis on the days of his youth in
Virginia.
      1. Jefferson, Thomas, 1743-1826—Childhood and youth—
Juvenile literature.   2. Presidents—United States—
Biography—Juvenile literature.   [1. Jefferson, Thomas,
1743-1826.   2. Presidents]   I. Baxter, Robert, 1930-
ill.   II. Title.
E332.27.S23   1986   973.4'6'0924 [B] [92]   85-1093
ISBN 0-8167-0561-5 (lib. bdg.)
ISBN 0-8167-0562-3 (pbk.)

Wa

Young
Thomas Jefferson

Some people are talented musicians. Some are brilliant writers. Others are great architects, inventors, political thinkers, or leaders. But in the long history of the world, only a few people have possessed *all* these skills. One of these extraordinary people was Thomas Jefferson.

Thomas Jefferson was born on April 13, 1743, in the colony of Virginia. The house in which Tom was born was called Shadwell. Shadwell was not like the great mansions built by rich plantation owners of that time. It was a simple, four-room, wooden house. The rooms were large and airy, and the house stood on a sturdy stone foundation. It was comfortable, and the Jefferson family loved it.

Peter Jefferson, Tom's father, was one of the first settlers to move into the western part of the Virginia Colony. This area was called the Piedmont. Piedmont means "at the foot of the mountain," and their home was just east of the Blue Ridge Mountains. Not many families lived in this region. Only a few farms dotted the forest lands. It was close enough to the frontier that Indians sometimes camped near the house and visited Tom's father.

The most important crop in Virginia was
tobacco, and many Virginia farmers grew rich
raising this crop. But that was in the Tidewater

area, a fertile flatland section near the Atlantic coast. Although tobacco was grown at Shadwell, the land was hilly, the soil poor. Even so, Peter and Jane Jefferson, and their children—Tom and his two older sisters, Jane and Mary—made their farm a success.

The beauty of Shadwell and the love he knew there stayed with Tom forever. Throughout his life, he kept coming back to the Piedmont. It was there, on a hill overlooking a beautiful river, that Tom later built his magnificent home, which he named Monticello.

Tom was two years old when the family left Shadwell. It was a sad but necessary move. Mrs. Jefferson's cousin, William Randolph, had suddenly died. Mr. Randolph's wife had died not long before, and the four Randolph children were now totally alone in the world. What's more, the huge Randolph estate, known as Tuckahoe, needed someone to run it. Everyone agreed that hard-working Peter Jefferson was the right man for the job.

There was no way for Mr. Jefferson to live at Shadwell and also take care of Tuckahoe. Seventy miles separated the two plantations, and in the eighteenth century it took three days to travel the distance on horseback. There was another good reason to move. Shadwell was too small a house for both the Jefferson family— which now included another daughter, Elizabeth —and the four Randolph children.

Tom enjoyed living at Tuckahoe. It was a big house filled with several bedrooms, a large parlor, and a dining room. There was room for many people at Tuckahoe, and guests visited often.

In those days when company came to dinner, they usually did not go home the same night. Traveling just took too long. For that reason visitors often remained at Tuckahoe for several days at a time.

All through the year there were formal dinners, hunting parties that lasted a week or more, and lively dances in the mansion parlor.

The house was often filled with many of Virginia's most respected citizens. For young Tom Jefferson, the activities at Tuckahoe were an important part of his education. Just by living there he learned good manners, how to dance and eat properly, and how to behave in company.

There were a number of children on the estate. To make sure they received a good education, Mr. Jefferson hired a teacher to set up a schoolroom. The teacher held classes in a small house near the mansion.

When Tom was five years old he also started classes with his sisters and cousins. As soon as he learned to print letters, he wrote his name on a schoolroom wall. Visitors today can still see the signature on the wall at Tuckahoe.

Tom attended the school for four years, learning reading, writing, and a small amount of arithmetic. If he had learned only that much, he still would have had as much education as most Virginians of that period. But Peter Jefferson, who never had any schooling himself, wanted more for his son. He knew Tom was a bright boy.

Even as a youngster, Tom Jefferson was interested in many subjects and kept careful records of everything that caught his attention. He wrote down the names of all the birds he saw on the plantation, and all the plants and animals in the area. He even listed the names of different insects in his notebooks.

Tom also learned the skills a colonial gentleman needed to know. He was taught to shoot and ride well, and not just for sport. Hunting game put food on the table, and riding a horse was the only way to travel. In many parts of Virginia it was impossible to use a carriage because there were no roads.

When Tom was nine years old, the Jefferson family moved back to Shadwell. The Randolph children were now old enough to take care of their property and no longer needed a guardian. Tom was placed in a school run by William Douglas, a clergyman from Scotland. Mr. Douglas was the preacher at Dover Church, five miles from Tuckahoe. His small school stood next to the church.

Tom lived at Mr. Douglas' school for four years. In that time he was taught the basics of Latin and Greek, as well as more English and mathematics. The math he learned was of great value to Thomas Jefferson in his adult life. As a young man he used mathematics when he

worked as a land surveyor, and later, when he laid out the designs for Monticello.

The subject Mr. Douglas taught best was French. Tom learned to read, write, and speak French well. Years later Thomas Jefferson would play a major part in French-American relations, first as a diplomat and then as President. Being able to speak with the French in their own language was a real advantage for Jefferson.

Tom spent his school holidays and vacations at Tuckahoe or Shadwell. But most of the school year, Tom lived at Reverend Douglas' home. For this, Mr. Jefferson paid nineteen pounds a year. That wasn't a huge fee, but it was more than many colonists earned in a year. Even so, it did not buy the kind of comforts to which Tom was accustomed. He looked forward to spending time at home or at Tuckahoe. It meant freedom and a chance to play. It also meant good meals, not just the small wedges of cold meat pie the students got at Reverend Douglas' table.

During vacations, Tom sometimes took short trips with his father. They often went into the wilderness west of the Allegheny Mountains. Mr. Jefferson, who was a part-time surveyor, liked exploring the forest lands. He drew maps of mountain passes and waterways, and charted territory for possible settlements. Tom's father was fascinated by the size of the continent. It seemed to stretch endlessly west.

Mr. Jefferson shared a great dream with his surveying partner and friend, Joshua Fry. Tom listened to their conversations and was caught up in their excitement. The dream was based on stories the two men had heard. They were told that there was a river in the west, with branches that flowed out into the Pacific Ocean. No one knew if the stories were true. But Jefferson and Fry wanted to be the ones to find the answer.

Their plan was to form a party of explorers and surveyors, and head west into the unknown territory. They hoped to find routes to the Pacific. But the plan ended in 1757, when Mr. Jefferson died at the age of forty-nine.

Tom never forgot his father's dream. He made it come true when he was President of the United States and commissioned the Lewis and Clark Expedition. Meriwether Lewis and William Clark led the group that did find a passage from the center of the continent to the Pacific Coast.

When Peter Jefferson died, Tom was just fourteen years old. He was far too young to run the family estate. Four close friends of his parents were named as guardians. They would look after the property for Mrs. Jefferson and her eight children. Then, when Tom reached the age of twenty-one, he would take on that responsibility.

One of the guardians' first decisions was that Tom should continue his education closer to home. He was sent to Reverend James Maury's small school, fourteen miles from Shadwell. Tom lived at the school but was now able to come home regularly.

Mr. Maury was an excellent teacher. He knew Greek and Latin far better than Mr. Douglas. He also taught geology, botany, and other natural sciences. During the next two years, Tom began reading such subjects as philosophy and government. Mr. Maury encouraged Tom to think about the relationship between people and their government. He helped Tom think about laws and rights and justice.

The late eighteenth century is often called the Age of Reason. It was a time when science and logic replaced superstition and other old-fashioned ways of thinking. Facts and hard evidence were now what mattered, and these came only from clear thinking.

Tom Jefferson was a child of his time. He grew up believing that answers to all the important questions would come through study, reason, and logic. He was certain that the only way to live a good, productive life was to find those answers.

Naturally, deep thinking took up only part of Tom's days. The tall, thin, red-headed teenager had endless energy, which he used in dozens of ways. He was a fine rider who delighted in having horse races with his cousins and school-mates.

Hunting was another of Tom's favorite pastimes, and he kept an exact record of every animal he shot. He listed its weight, size, color, and every other fact he considered worthwhile.

26

It was typical of young Tom Jefferson to pay close attention to these details, and to write them down. This was a practice that stayed with him for the rest of his life.

It was also during his years at Mr. Maury's school that Tom began taking violin lessons. Playing the violin became another passion that stayed with him throughout his life. From the first day he learned to play the instrument, Tom practiced it two or three hours daily. Whether practicing the violin, riding his horse, studying nature or French or math, Tom Jefferson did it wholeheartedly.

Sometimes it seemed funny to Dabney Carr, Tom's best friend, that Tom filled every minute of every day with activity. For example, the boys liked to walk through the woods after Mr. Maury's classes were over. Dabney did it to relax. But Tom took the opportunity to observe the birds, the condition of the trees and shrubs, and everything else that caught his eye or ear.

In the fall of 1759, Dabney told Tom that this would be his last year at Mr. Maury's school. That coming spring, Dabney was going off to study at William and Mary College, in Williamsburg, Virginia. It was a fine college, but

Dabney was interested in more than schooling. He told Tom that Williamsburg was an exciting place. There were dances every night, dinners, parties, plays, and concerts. Furthermore, Dabney said that the best and smartest people of Virginia went there.

Tom instantly wanted to go to Williamsburg with his friend. He hoped his guardians would give him permission to go. To get that permission, Tom knew his request had to make very good sense. So he carefully thought out his reasons for wanting to go to William and Mary.

First, he wrote in a letter, many young people visited him at Shadwell. This, of course, kept him from his studies. It also cost a great deal of money for the family to feed and take care of those guests. If he were away at college, Tom's letter went on, the estate would not have to spend so much money entertaining company.

Tom's second reason was that, in Williamsburg, he would get to meet people who would be of help to him in the future.

Finally, he pointed out, he could take more advanced studies in Greek, Latin, and mathematics.

31

Tom's guardians agreed that he would benefit a great deal from going to college and living in Williamsburg. As a future gentleman and landowner, Tom would be expected to take part in governing the colony of Virginia. Therefore, he needed to learn more about the entire colony, not just his area. He also needed to take part in adult society. The guardians knew that only by living in the capital of Virginia could Tom learn to work with all kinds of situations and people. They granted their permission.

The people of Jefferson's time considered Williamsburg a large city. The town had about two hundred houses and one thousand people. The streets, which were unpaved, were laid out in straight lines. They ran from east to west and from north to south. No street in Williamsburg curved or went off at an angle.

In the center of town there was a large, open square, with trees and walking paths. Running right through the center of the square was Williamsburg's main street. It was so wide that many carriages could travel it at the same time. This broad street stretched for three quarters of a mile. At one end stood the capitol building of Virginia. At the other end stood the College of William and Mary.

Thomas Jefferson was almost seventeen years old when he arrived in Williamsburg. It was the spring of 1760 and the capital was having its busiest season. The Virginia legislature, called the House of Burgesses, held its meeting there every spring. "Burgess" was the name for an elected representative in Virginia. The General Court also met there, as did the Governor's council. Spring also brought plantation families into town for shopping, business, and social events. All winter the cold weather and bad roads kept them at home.

William and Mary College in 1760 was not like the colleges of today. It was divided into four schools. There was a grammar school for boys fourteen and younger. The school Jefferson entered was the school of philosophy. There was also a school of divinity, for students who wanted to become clergymen. Finally, there was a school for American Indians. Altogether, the college had about one hundred students and six teachers.

Tom was disappointed in his classes. Because he had read so much and learned so well in his earlier schools, Tom was way ahead of his classmates. He also found it hard to keep his mind on his studies. So much was going on in the town! Soon he and Dabney Carr were enjoying the nonstop social life around them.

In his first year at college, Tom spent more money than he should have. He bought a whole wardrobe of new clothes. He ordered fine saddles, bridles, and other supplies for the horses he kept in a stable near the school. As a result, Tom found himself in debt by the end of the school year.

Tom didn't have enough money to cover his debts. He had to write to one of his guardians to ask for help. But he was so ashamed of wasting money that he asked that the bills be paid from

his part of the family estate. He felt that his brother and sisters should not have to share the cost of his foolishness.

When Tom's guardian saw the bills and read the letter, he smiled understandingly. It was clear to him that the young man had learned his lesson and didn't need a lecture or punishment. He wrote to Tom, "If you have sowed your wild oats in this way, the estate can well afford to pay the bill." The guardian's letter also suggested that Tom avoid making the same mistake again.

In his second year at William and Mary, Tom had little time for foolishness. His schoolwork was more demanding than it had been the first year. The new head of the school of philosophy, Dr. William Small, saw that young Tom Jefferson was unusually intelligent, and needed only to be wisely guided. Dr. Small made sure that Tom read widely in poetry, philosophy, history, Greek, Latin, French, and science. He also encouraged Tom to use the equipment in the William and Mary laboratory.

The college had the best-equipped laboratory in the colonies. It contained barometers, telescopes, lenses, and many other scientific instruments. Tom's scientific studies set the groundwork for his later success as an inventor. Among his inventions were a mechanical letter-writer, a dumbwaiter (a kind of elevator for transporting objects from one floor to another), a clock that told both the time and the day of the week, a more efficient plow, and a furnace that heated an entire house with warm air.

During Tom's second year at college he developed patterns of work and study that he would follow for the rest of his life. He awoke every morning at dawn to begin studying. The day was divided into class hours, meals, more study, exercise, and still more study before going to sleep at 2:00 A.M.

Tom also spent three to four hours each day practicing his violin. Despite all that work, he found time to be with friends, attend an occasional party, and take part in a string

quartet. At about this point in his life, Tom began to keep a daily diary. In it, he noted how his days progressed and what he accomplished. This was Tom's way of making sure that he didn't fall into lazy habits.

41

After his second year at William and Mary, the nineteen-year-old left college to study law with a man named George Wythe. Mr. Wythe was one of the most important lawyers in Virginia.

Jefferson's friends considered him lucky to be given a clerkship with George Wythe.

There were no law schools in those days. Someone who wanted to become a lawyer had to work for an attorney, read law books, and learn as much as possible. Then, after a few years, the young clerk would be tested by a group of attorneys. If he did well in this examination, he was accepted into the practice of law.

The five years that Tom Jefferson spent studying law with Mr. Wythe proved to be extremely important in his future, and in the future of the country. In addition to learning as much as he could about English and Colonial law, he studied Anglo-Saxon. That is the language in which England's original laws were written. Knowing Anglo-Saxon helped Jefferson learn how some laws came to be, and what they told about the relationship between rulers and the people they ruled. This was a serious matter in Colonial America. It was, in fact, one of the issues that led to the American Revolution.

Some colonists, such as Jefferson's friend, Patrick Henry, believed that England's king was taking away rights that belonged to the Colonies. Other colonists did not agree. They said that the only rights the colonists had were those given by the king. They believed the king could also take away those rights. It was this disagreement that lay behind many of the cases that were tried in colonial courts, and much of the argument about colonial taxes.

As Jefferson studied the laws of his time, and the origins of those laws, he began to change his thinking. Raised as a colonial gentlemen and an English subject, he had been taught to believe in and obey the king and the English government. Now he was beginning to think like an American. He began to believe that certain rights belonged to the people. These rights, he would argue in the Declaration of Independence, are not the king's to give or to take. Jefferson was also coming to believe that a king who abuses the rights of the people deserves to lose their loyalty.

Whereas in

Following his five years with Mr. Wythe, Thomas Jefferson became a lawyer, at the age of twenty-four. He continued to practice law until the courts were closed at the beginning of the American Revolution. During those years he also served as a member of the Virginia House of Burgesses. As a Burgess, Tom was not a first-rate speaker like Patrick Henry. But he gained everyone's respect for his clear and brilliant writing on legal and governmental matters.

This good reputation led the Continental Congress, of which he was a member, to ask Jefferson to write a Declaration of Independence. If he had done nothing else in his lifetime, Jefferson would deserve his nation's praise and admiration for this important document. It united the colonies, and gave purpose to the fight that would end in the creation of a new nation.

However, Jefferson's career contained many more remarkable achievements. He served in the Virginia State Legislature. There, he helped to write important laws, such as the bill for establishing religious freedom. This would become the model for the idea of religious freedom in the American Constitution.

Jefferson also served his state as governor for two terms. He went on to serve his country as a member of Congress, as U.S. Minister to France, as Secretary of State, and as third President of the United States.

Thomas Jefferson lived eighty-three years. In that time, he left his mark on almost every area of American life, and he was much loved and honored by his fellow citizens. The name of Thomas Jefferson will forever be linked to the birth of the United States on July 4, 1776. And, ironically, it was on the fiftieth anniversary of that momentous day—July 4, 1826—that Thomas Jefferson died.